Avi

My Favorite Writer

Leia Tait

Published by Weigl Publishers Inc.
350 5th Avenue, Suite 3304, PMB 6G
New York, NY 10118-0069

Web site: www.weigl.com
Copyright ©2007 WEIGL PUBLISHERS INC.

Library of Congress Cataloging-in-Publication Data

Tait, Leia.
  Avi / Leia Tait.
      p. cm. -- (My favorite writer)
  Includes index.
  ISBN 1-59036-478-3 (lib. bdg. : alk. paper) -- ISBN 1-59036-479-1
(pbk. : alk. paper)
  1. Avi, 1937---Juvenile literature. 2. Authors, American--20th century--
Biography--Juvenile literature. 3. Children's stories--Authorship--Juvenile
literature. I. Title. II. Series.
  PS3551.V5Z87 2007
  813'.54--dc22
  [B]

                                                    2006016144

Printed in the United States of America
1 2 3 4 5 6 7 8 9 0 09 08 07 06 05

Project Coordinator
Heather C. Hudak

Design
Terry Paulhus

All of the Internet URLs given in the book were valid at the time of
publication. However, due to the dynamic nature of the Internet, some
addresses may have changed, or sites may have ceased to exist since
publication. While the author and publisher regret any inconvenience this
may cause readers, no responsibility for any such changes can be accepted
by either the author or the publisher.

Contents

Avi

MILESTONES

1937 Born December 23 in New York City

1955 Decides to become a writer; graduates from high school and enters Antioch College in Ohio

1956 Transfers to the University of Wisconsin

1960 Wins playwriting contest

1963 Marries Joan Gainer

1970 Publishes first book; becomes a librarian at Trenton State College

1986 Marries Coppélia Kahn

1987 Moves to Rhode Island; becomes a full-time writer

1996 Marries Linda Wright; moves to Denver, Colorado

2003 Publishes 50th book; wins Newbery Medal

Avi Wortis has been writing children's books for more than 36 years. He has written more than 60 books. His stories are full of action and suspense. They are also known for their realistic settings and characters. Avi's heroes and heroines face the same challenges that real young people face. They teach children how to make wise decisions and remain true to themselves.

Avi is an unusual author because he writes books in several genres. A genre is a type, or category, of book. Avi writes mysteries, adventure stories, and fantasies. Some of his books are picture books. Others are animal tales, which Avi has enjoyed since he was a child. Many of Avi's books are **historical novels**. These are popular with his readers, and they have won many awards. Avi's ability to write well in so many genres sets him apart from other authors. It also means that many young people have enjoyed at least one of his books.

No matter what kinds of books Avi writes, they are always interesting, exciting, and meaningful. Avi says that he loves writing for children.

Early Childhood

Avi was born in New York City on December 23, 1937. His twin sister, Emily, was born five minutes later. Their brother, Henry, was already 2 years old. During his first year of life, Avi had a different name. Today, he keeps that name a secret. It was not his for very long. When Avi and Emily were about a year old, Emily tried to say her twin brother's name. What came out was "Avi" (pronounced AH-vee). His family decided they liked this name much better than the one he already had. He has been called Avi ever since.

Avi's childhood home was full of books. He learned to read at a very young age. During the day, Avi and his siblings read to themselves. Each night, their mother read to them before bed. In Avi's family, writing was both a **pastime** and a **profession**. Two of his great-grandfathers were writers. One of his grandmothers wrote plays and published a **memoir.** Writing was also an important part of his parents' professional lives. His father, Joseph, was a **psychiatrist**. He wrote papers about his theories and **research**. Avi's mother, Helen, was a social worker. She also wrote articles about her work. Helen published short stories and folk tales, too. Avi came to value reading and writing naturally.

Avi was raised in Brooklyn, a New York City borough.

6

In 1941, when Avi was 4 years old, Japan bombed Pearl Harbor, Hawaii. When this happened, the United States entered World War II. The war affected Avi in many ways. His father went to work for the U.S. Coast Guard. He helped sailors deal with the stresses of war. Avi helped the war effort by collecting scrap metal and old newspapers for recycling. At night, the government imposed **blackouts**. This meant that the whole city had to be kept dark. The blackouts made it harder for enemy pilots to see where the cities were located.

In his free time, Avi liked to play games with his friends. One of his favorite games was punch ball. This was like baseball, except instead of hitting the ball with a bat, Avi and his friends punched it with their fists. They also loved to build things from scraps of wood. Sometimes, Avi would build wooden airplanes. Other times, he and his friends would build huge forts. They loved to make up clubs and play games that let them use their imagination. Avi also enjoyed art. He had taken art classes at the Brooklyn Children's Museum when he was a child.

With a population of more than 8 million people, New York is the largest city in the United States.

Growing Up

Avi's difficulties in school sometimes made him feel like a failure.

Avi began elementary school in 1942. He did well in science. It was his favorite class. Avi loved airplanes and wanted to design them one day. Other than science, Avi was not interested in school. He found it boring. He also had trouble with writing. He often misspelled words. Sometimes he did not notice that he had put the wrong letters in a word. For example, when he tried to write *soup*, it came out as *soap*. Sometimes, he would spell a word correctly in one sentence and incorrectly in the next. Other times, Avi would leave whole words out of sentences or add extra words where they did not belong. When he was an adult, Avi learned that he has "symptoms of dysgraphia." Dysgraphia makes it hard for some people to write clearly. It also makes it difficult for them to see their mistakes.

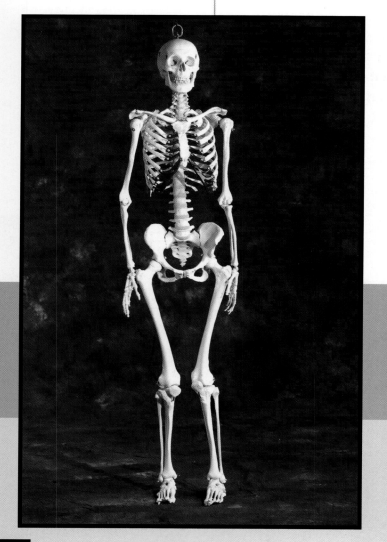

As a child, Avi enjoyed science. He was very interested in a human skeleton that a renter kept in his family's home.

These symptoms made school difficult for Avi. He earned fairly good grades, but he did not think he was a good student. He often felt frustrated and upset. No matter how hard he tried, he could not improve his writing. His teachers did not know about his symptoms of dysgraphia. They did not understand why he made the mistakes he did. Avi knew he was trying his best, but nothing seemed to help. To make matters worse, Avi's twin sister, Emily, was an excellent student. She often earned perfect scores on spelling tests. Until eighth grade, the twins were always in the same class together. Avi was often compared to his sister, which upset him. His older brother, Henry, did very well in school, too. Henry was so bright that he went to college when he was only 15 years old. Avi's writing problems made him feel different from the rest of his family.

Inspired to Write

During World War II, New York City suffered a housing shortage. To help out, Avi's parents rented out a room in their house. One of the people who stayed with Avi's family during this time was a medical student. As part of his studies, he kept a real human skeleton in his room. This fascinated the Wortis children. When Avi became an adult, he created a character based on the medical student in his book, *Who Was That Masked Man, Anyway?*

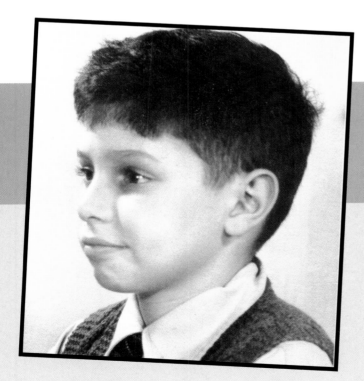

■ When he was young, Avi did not know why his writing was so poor.

Avi began high school in 1951. His parents let him choose which school he wanted to attend. Avi chose Stuyvesant High School in Manhattan. It was the same school his brother had attended. Stuyvesant was a large school with more than 5,000 students. All of the students were boys. In his first 6 weeks there, Avi failed all of his classes. His parents were very concerned. They moved him to a much smaller school called Elisabeth Irwin High School. This school focused on writing. The teachers helped Avi a great deal.

Avi liked his new school, but he continued to struggle with his writing. Finally, one of his teachers suggested that he get extra help. Avi's parents found him a tutor. Her name was Ella Ratner. She gave Avi hope. She helped him see that even though his writing skills were weak, his ideas were good. Ella knew that Avi was creative but had trouble sharing his ideas. She told Avi that if he could learn to write better, people would know how interesting he was. When Avi heard this, he felt much better. He wanted people to know about his ideas. He decided to become a writer.

At Elisabeth Irwin High School, students can study the arts, such as writing and painting.

Avi set his hopes on becoming a playwright. A playwright is someone who writes plays. Like many writers, Avi began keeping a diary. In his diary, Avi made a list of all the books he read. He outlined plays he was working on and jotted down ideas for essays he wanted to write. Keeping a diary helped Avi practice his writing every day. Even though Avi was not able to fix his symptoms of dysgraphia, he found ways to manage them. His confidence grew. Avi became more determined to become a writer after high school.

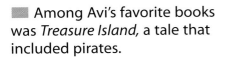 Among Avi's favorite books was *Treasure Island,* a tale that included pirates.

As a teenager, Avi enjoyed reading a variety of books.

Favorite Books

As a child, Avi's favorite activity was reading. He received at least one book for every birthday. He also used his own money to buy books for himself. As a young child, Avi's favorite books were animal stories. He enjoyed *The Wind in the Willows* and *Otto the Giant Dog.* Another of his favorite tales was *Freddie the Pig Travels.* As he grew older, Avi read more adventure stories, including the Tom Swift series by Victor Appleton. He also enjoyed the science fiction novels of Jules Verne, including *Twenty Thousand Leagues Under the Sea.* His favorite book was *Treasure Island,* by Robert Louis Stevenson. Today, Avi names Stevenson, Ernest Hemingway, and Charles Dickens as the authors who have influenced him the most. Reading these authors, Avi has said, makes him want to write the best that he can.

Learning the Craft

In the fall of 1955, Avi went to Yellow Springs, Ohio, to attend Antioch College. A year later, he transferred to the University of Wisconsin. He studied history and theater. Avi's love of history began in his childhood. All of his grandparents had moved to the United States from different places in Europe. Each loved to tell stories about life in the "old country," as they called it. Avi's **paternal** grandfather also enjoyed telling stories from U.S. history. The stories helped Avi understand why his grandparents came to the United States.

In his free time, Avi continued to write plays. When he finished his history degree in 1959, he stayed on at the university to study playwriting. While he was there, the university held a playwriting contest. Avi decided to enter. He wrote a play about the American Revolution. It was called *A Little Rebellion*. Avi's play won first prize in the competition. After Avi won, two different magazines published his play. The University of Wisconsin also **produced** the play. Avi was very proud. Eventually, Avi earned a master of arts degree in theater.

While in college, Avi studied history, a subject he had been interested in since childhood.

Avi learned about history and theater at the University of Wisconsin.

In 1960, Avi moved to San Francisco and wrote plays for the World Theatre. Although Avi kept this job for a year, none of his plays were produced. Avi felt discouraged. He decided to move back to New York. There, Avi worked as a sign-maker, a carpenter, and a drama coach. He continued to write plays. While working as a drama coach, Avi met a young dance coach named Joan Gainer. They began dating and later married.

One day, Avi saw an ad for a job that interested him. The New York Public Library needed a clerk for its theater collection. Avi applied and got the job.

Clerking for the library's theater collection was perfect for Avi. Avi enjoyed his new job so much that he began taking evening classes in **library science** at Columbia University. In 1964, Avi earned a second master of arts degree, this time in library science.

Avi and Joan had their first child, Shaun, in 1966. Two years later, their second son, Kevin, was born. Avi loved being a father.

Inspired to Write

Avi never thought of writing for children until his own sons were born. They opened up a whole new world to Avi. Being a parent allowed Avi to be part of the world of children. His sons inspired Avi to write good books. They showed Avi the joy a good book can bring. For this reason, Avi has said that his children gave him his profession.

For a time, Avi worked as a clerk at the New York Public Library.

Getting Published

"It was only when my eldest son, Shaun, was born, that I took to writing for kids. Since then, I've never written anything else."
Avi

Once he had children, Avi looked for ways to earn extra money to support his family. In 1968, he decided to **illustrate** greeting cards. Avi showed them to his friends and family. One of his friends had just written a children's book. When she saw Avi's illustrations, she asked him to draw the pictures for her book. Avi agreed. Avi's friend took the book to a **publishing company**. An **editor** there became interested in Avi's drawings. She asked him to write and illustrate a book of his own.

Avi decided to write about a game that he and his 2-year-old son, Shaun, often played. When Shaun wanted Avi to make up a tale, he would point to an object around the house and say, "Tell me a story." Then Avi would create a story involving that object. Avi thought that if Shaun liked these stories, perhaps other children would like them, too. He wrote down all the stories he could remember telling. Then he drew pictures to go with each story. Avi's **agent** took the finished book back to the publishing company. After reading it, the editor decided not to publish

The Publishing Process

Publishing companies receive hundreds of **manuscripts** from authors each year. Only a few manuscripts become books. Publishers must be sure that a manuscript will sell many copies. As a result, publishers reject most of the manuscripts they receive.

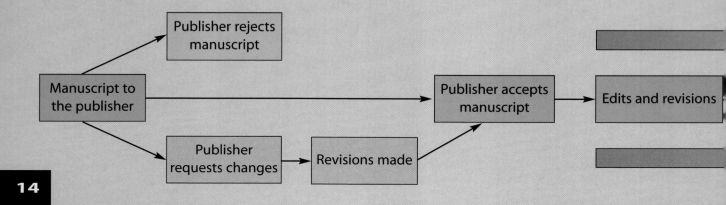

Avi's book. His agent took the book to other publishers. Eventually, one company decided it liked Avi's book enough to publish it, but only if someone else did the illustrations. In 1970, Avi's book was finally published. It was called *Things That Sometimes Happen: Thirty Very Short Stories for Very Young Readers.*

Avi quit his job at the New York Public Library and moved to Trenton, New Jersey. He became a librarian at Trenton State College. For the next 17 years, Avi worked as a librarian during the day and wrote books for children at night and on weekends.

In 1975, Avi wrote his first novel for young people. It was called *No More Magic.* Avi has published at least one book per year since then.

Avi married his second wife, Coppélia Kahn, in 1986. Four years later, Avi quit his job as a librarian at Trenton State College. He and Coppélia moved to Providence, Rhode Island, and Avi became a full-time writer.

Inspired to Write

When Avi moved to Rhode Island in 1987, his new home influenced his writing. Rhode Island is the setting for many of Avi's books. Living in a large house full of nooks and crannies, Avi began to imagine a ghost story. This story became Avi's book *Something Upstairs.*

Once a manuscript has been accepted, it goes through many stages before it is published. Often, authors change their work to follow an editor's suggestions. Once the book is published, some authors receive royalties. This is money based on book sales.

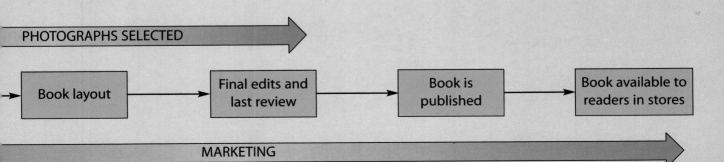

PHOTOGRAPHS SELECTED →

Book layout → Final edits and last review → Book is published → Book available to readers in stores

MARKETING →

Writer Today

Avi has published more than 60 children's books. He is best known for his historical novels. *The True Confessions of Charlotte Doyle* won a Newbery Honor Award in 1991, and *Crispin: The Cross of Lead* won the Newbery Medal in 2003. The Newbery Medal is the most important prize in children's literature. Avi has said that winning the Newbery Medal made him feel "surprised, elated, humbled, and deeply moved."

Avi's books have also won many other awards, such as the *Boston Globe-Horn Book* Award, the Scott O'Dell Award, the Golden Kite Award, and a Mystery Writers of America Special Award. As a result, Avi is a highly respected author.

■ Avi lives with his family in Denver, Colorado.

In 1996, Avi moved to Denver, Colorado. He lives there with his third wife, Linda Wright, and his stepchildren. Avi continues to write every day. He has an office where he types his books on a computer. The built-in spell-check helps Avi manage his symptoms of dysgraphia.

Avi often begins writing at 5 or 6 o'clock in the morning. He likes to work in complete silence. He usually writes for about five hours a day. When he is not writing, Avi spends most of his time with his family. He also has several hobbies. Avi enjoys photography. He likes cooking and listening to all kinds of music. He rarely watches television. Avi still finds time to read, and he enjoys daydreaming, just like when he was a child.

Growing up, Avi's son Shaun loved to listen to his father make up stories.

Popular Books

A vi has been writing children's books for more than 36 years. Here are some of his most popular novels.

AWARDS
Something Upstairs

1989 Named One of the Best Books of the Year by the Library of Congress

1991 Rhode Island Children's Book Award

1992 Sunshine State Young Reader's Award (Florida)

1993 California Young Readers Award

Something Upstairs

In *Something Upstairs*, Avi combines historical fiction, mystery, horror, and science fiction to create a tale of suspense. Kenny Huldorf is a 12-year-old boy who has recently moved to Providence, Rhode Island. His new home was built in the eighteenth century. Kenny's room in the attic has a strange stain on the floor. One day, Kenny finds himself face-to-face with Caleb, the ghost of a slave murdered in the house 200 years before. Caleb appears to Kenny repeatedly. He begs Kenny to solve his murder.

While doing research at the local library, Kenny meets the evil Pardon Willinghast, who seems to have a secret. One night, Caleb takes Kenny back in time to the night of his murder. Kenny is shocked to find Willinghast waiting for them. He soon learns that he is not the first to try to help Caleb. Willinghast has stopped everyone else. Kenny is given a frightening choice: kill Caleb, or remain trapped in the past forever.

NEWBERY HONOR AWARD-WINNING AUTHOR

AVON CAMELOT

Avi

SOMETHING UPSTAIRS

"A SPOOKY, INGENIOUS TREAT FOR GHOST-STORY FANS." *Kirkus Reviews*

The True Confessions of Charlotte Doyle

More than 25 years after being published, *The True Confessions of Charlotte Doyle* remains one of Avi's most popular books. In 1832, 13-year-old Charlotte Doyle must travel from Britain to Rhode Island aboard a ship called the Seahawk. Upon boarding, Charlotte is alarmed to find that she is the only female, in fact the only passenger, on board. At first, she seeks the protection of the ship's Captain Jaggery. Then she discovers that he is a cruel and unstable man. She then joins the ship's crew, who are planning to mutiny against Captain Jaggery. Charlotte helps the crew in its difficult and dangerous work of keeping the ship afloat. By doing so, she changes from a prim and proper young lady to a strong and able shipmate. Enraged by her betrayal, Captain Jaggery accuses Charlotte of murder. He has her put on trial and found guilty. Charlotte defends her life against Jaggery. Eventually, she arrives in Rhode Island, where she must make a difficult choice between her old life with her family and her newfound love of the sea.

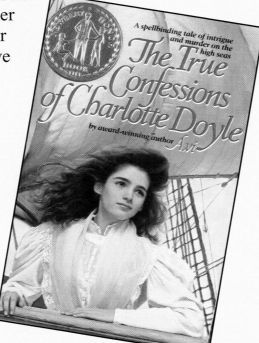

AWARD
The True Confessions of Charlotte Doyle

1990 One of the Best Books of the Year, *School Library Journal*

1990 Best Books for Teens, New York Public Library

1990 Children's Choice Award, International Reading Association

1991 Notable Children's Trade Book in the Language Arts

1991 Newbery Honor Book

1991 *Boston Globe-Horn Book* Award

1991 *Horn Book*'s Fanfare Award

1991 *English Journal*'s Honor List

1992 ALA Notable Children's Book

1994 Sunshine State Young Readers Award (Florida)

1994 Beehive Award, Children's Literature Association of Utah

1996 Massachusetts Children's Choice Award

2000 Named One of the 100 Most Significant Children's Books in the 20th Century by the *School Library Journal*

Nothing But the Truth

Nothing But the Truth is what is called a "documentary novel." This means that a narrator does not tell the story. Instead, the reader pieces the story together from character conversations, diary entries, letters, talk-show transcripts, school memos, dialogue, and newspaper articles. The tale that unfolds revolves around Philip Malloy. Phillip finds himself caught in a scandal after he hums along with the national anthem at school. His teacher, Miss Narwin, punishes him for causing a disturbance. Philip in turn accuses her of being **antipatriotic**. The school becomes involved, and then so does the **media**. The situation quickly gets out of control. The truth of what happened becomes muddled. Like a detective, the reader must review the evidence and decide what really happened. The novel's format and its message about truth have made it a favorite of young readers.

Poppy

In *Poppy*, Avi creates an animal tale like those he loved as a child. Poppy is a **dormouse** who lives with her family and friends in Dimwood Forest. Ruling over Dimwood is Ocax, a hoot owl who promises to protect the mice from a local porcupine. In return, the mice must be completely obedient to Ocax. Poppy goes along with this agreement until she sees Ocax eat her fiancé, Ragweed. Ocax also denies her family's request to move to a new home. Upset, Poppy embarks on a dangerous quest to reveal Ocax's true nature. Along the way, she has a number of adventures. In the end, Poppy must battle Ocax one-on-one. The true heroine in her emerges. The book's likable characters and action-packed plot have made *Poppy* a very popular book. Avi enjoyed writing the book so much that he has created more books set in Dimwood Forest. These include *Poppy and Rye* (1998), *Ragweed* (1999), *Ereth's Birthday* (2000), and *Poppy's Return* (2005).

Crispin: The Cross of Lead

Crispin: The Cross of Lead was Avi's 50th book. It won the Newbery Medal, the biggest prize in children's writing. The story is set in fourteenth-century Britain. It follows Crispin, a 13-year-old peasant boy whose mother has just died. On the back of her most treasured piece of jewelry, a lead cross, Crispin finds some mysterious words. Before he can learn what they mean from the village priest, the man is murdered. Astonishingly, Crispin is accused of the crime. He is declared a wanted criminal. Crispin flees to save his life. Eventually, he meets a travelling juggler, who takes him under his wing. As the story continues, Crispin finds himself fighting the unfairness of **feudalism**. He also learns his true identity. In the end, Crispin is able to claim his rightful place in the world. Many people have praised the book for its entertaining characters and for showing events during this time in history as they really happened.

AWARDS

Poppy

1995 Named among Best Books of the Year at the New York Public Library

1995 Named One of the Best Books of the Year by the *School Library Journal*

1995 Named among Best Books of the Year by *Booklist*

1996 Named ALA Notable Book

1996 *Boston Globe-Horn Book* Award Best Fiction

1998 Maryland Children's Choice Award

1999 Land of Enchantment Book Award (New Mexico)

Crispin: The Cross of Lead

2003 Newbery Medal

2003 ALA Notable Children's Books

2003 Named among Best Children's Books of the Year by Bank Street College of Education

2003 Colorado Book Award

2003 Named to *Book Sense* Top Ten

Creative Writing Tips

Avi had to work very hard to become a writer. Due to his dysgraphia, writing never came easily for him. Although Avi still struggles with this disorder today, he has found many ways to manage his symptoms and improve his writing. Many of these strategies are useful practices for any writer. Here are some tips that might help you become a better writer.

Practice

Writing stories is different than just telling stories, and it takes practice. Take time to write something every single day, even if it is only a few paragraphs. Writing every day will help you develop a routine and will teach you how you work best. Try keeping a journal. Every night, write down an event that happened to you during the day. Describe each event as if you were writing a story for someone.

Avi is able to make up interesting stories about everyday objects or things found around his home.

Rewrite

The first **draft** of anything you write should never be the last. Most writers make several drafts before they are finished. Your first draft should get you started. Once you have completed it, reread what you have written. What things do you like about it? What can you improve? Have you fully explained everything? Are your ideas clear? Are they connected to one another? Are the words you have chosen descriptive? Each time you rewrite, focus on specific things you want to improve. Try reading your work aloud to help you hear what you have written. Rewrite as many times as necessary.

Write for a Reader

Always remember that someone else will read your writing. Even if you understand what you have written, your reader may not. Keep this in mind while you are writing. Avi writes books for many different audiences. He believes that the job of a writer is to make the reader understand what he or she is trying to say. His books for very young children are different in content, structure, and style than those he writes for older children.

Read

Writers learn about writing from the books they read, and most writers read a great deal. It is important for writers to read various kinds of books by many different authors. As a child, Avi read three or four books a week. He has said that reading is the key to good writing. Reading many books will help you learn what kinds of stories you like best. Visit libraries and bookstores. Ask teachers, librarians, and booksellers for suggestions.

Inspired to Write

Avi is often asked, "Where do you get your ideas?" He believes everyone has ideas. Avi turns his ideas into stories. He makes connections between unrelated pieces of his life, such as random thoughts, conversations, and events. Alone, each of these things might not mean much. Linked together, however, they can form a story.

Reading different kinds of books by a variety of authors can help you become a better writer.

Writing a Biography Review

A biography is an account of an individual's life that is written by another person. Some people's lives are very interesting. In school, you may be asked to write a biography review. The first thing to do when writing a biography review is to decide whom you would like to learn about. Your school library or community library will have a large selection of biographies from which to choose.

Are you interested in an author, a sports figure, an inventor, a movie star, or a president? Finding the right book is your first task. Whether you choose to write your review on a biography of Avi or another person, the task will be similar.

Begin your review by writing the title of the book, the author, and the person featured in the book. Then, start writing about the main events in the person's life. Include such things as where the person grew up and what his or her childhood was like. You will want to add details about the person's adult life, such as whether he or she married or had children. Next, write about what you think makes this person special. What kinds of experiences influenced this individual? For instance, did he or she grow up in unusual circumstances? Was the person determined to accomplish a goal? Include any details that surprised you. A concept web is a useful research tool. Use the concept web on the right to begin researching your biography review.

- Where does the individual currently reside?
- Does he or she have a family?
- Does he or she have children or grandchildren?

- What did you learn from the book?
- Would you recommend the book to others?
- Was anything missing from the book?

- Where and when was the individual born?
- Describe the individual's parents, siblings, and friends.
- Did the person grow up in unusual circumstances?

Your Opinion

Adulthood

Childhood

REVIEWING A BIOGRAPHY

Main Accomplishments

Help and Obstacles

Work and Preparation

- What is the individual's life's work?
- Has he or she received awards or recognition for accomplishments?
- How have the person's accomplishments served others?

- What was the individual's education?
- What was his or her work experience?
- How does this person work; what is the process?

- Did the individual have a positive attitude?
- Did he or she receive assistance from others?
- Did the individual have a mentor?

25

Fan Information

Avi loves to meet his fans. When he is not writing, one of Avi's favorite things to do is to visit libraries and schools. There, he talks to children about his books. He explains his writing process, holds writing workshops, and reads from his books. Avi particularly enjoys reading to children from books he has not yet finished. This helps him figure out what parts of the book his readers like and which parts need improvement. During these visits, Avi makes a point of talking with children who struggle in school just as he did. He brings along copies of his manuscripts to show them his spelling mistakes and his editors' corrections in red ink. Avi hopes that this helps students understand that they do not have to be perfect to do great things.

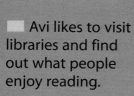 Avi likes to visit libraries and find out what people enjoy reading.

Avi also enjoys receiving fan mail. He receives many letters from readers who have enjoyed his books. He thinks getting letters from fans is one of the most rewarding things about being a writer. "The nicest compliment I ever got," says Avi, "was from a kid who wrote me a letter saying this and that and the last line was, 'thank you for putting another book in the world.' That says it all, doesn't it? 'Thank you.'"

Avi's fans also can enjoy his stories in other forms. In 1997, *Something Upstairs* was made into a play and performed by the Louisville Children's Theater. *Something Upstairs*, *Night Journeys*, *Sometimes I Think I Hear My Name*, and *City of Light, City of Dark* have all been purchased by film companies to be turned into movies. Work has already begun on a movie version of *The True Confessions of Charlotte Doyle*.

To learn more about Avi's upcoming projects, his past books, and his life as a writer, fans can visit Avi's personal website. Here, Avi provides a list of all his titles, along with descriptions of each book and his personal reasons for writing them. There is a biography, some advice for young writers, and answers to commonly asked questions. Fans can even read Avi's Newbery Medal acceptance speech.

WEB LINKS

Avi's Official Website

www.avi-writer.com

Visitors to Avi's official website will learn all about Avi and his books. The site includes a biography, Avi's tips for good writing, a list of Avi's published books, and answers to frequently asked questions.

Greenville Public Library

www.yourlibrary.ws

Click on "Kids and Teens," then "Authors of the Month." Click on "Avi" under December. This Web page provides a biography of Avi and a list of his books, each with a short description of the story.

Quiz

1

Q: What was the title of Avi's first book?

A: *Things That Sometimes Happen: Thirty Very Short Stories for Very Young Readers*

2

Q: What year was Avi's first book published?

A: 1970

3

Q: When did Avi publish his first novel?

A: 1975

Q: What was the name of Avi's high school?

A: Elisabeth Irwin High School

Q: What are some of Avi's hobbies?

A: Cooking, photography, listening to music, reading, and daydreaming

Q: What did Avi study in university?

A: History, theater, and library science

Q: What was the name of Avi's tutor?

A: Ella Ratner

Q: What was Avi's favorite subject in elementary school?

A: Science

Q: Where does Avi live today?

A: Denver, Colorado

Q: When did Avi win the Newbery Medal, and for which book?

A: In 2003, for *Crispin: The Cross of Lead*

29

Writing Terms

This glossary will introduce you to some of the main terms in the field of writing. Understanding these common writing terms will allow you to discuss your ideas about books and writing with others.

action: the moving events of a work of fiction

antagonist: the person in the story who opposes the main character

autobiography: a history of a person's life written by that person

biography: a written account of another person's life

character: a person in a story, poem, or play

climax: the most exciting moment or turning point in a story

episode: a short piece of action, or scene, in a story

fiction: stories about characters and events that are not real

foreshadow: hinting at something that is going to happen later in the book

imagery: a written description of a thing or idea that brings an image to mind

narrator: the speaker of the story who relates the events

nonfiction: writing that deals with real people and events

novel: published writing of considerable length that portrays characters within a story

plot: the order of events in a work of fiction

protagonist: the leading character of a story; often a likable character

resolution: the end of the story, when the conflict is settled

scene: a single episode in a story

setting: the place and time in which a work of fiction occurs

theme: an idea that runs throughout a work of fiction

Glossary

agent: somebody who officially represents somebody else in business

antipatriotic: disliking others' love of their country

blackouts: when the lights go out in large areas because electrical power is turned off

dormouse: a rodent that looks like a small squirrel

draft: an early version of a piece of writing

editor: someone who obtains and improves the content of a book, magazine, or newspaper

feudalism: the legal and social system that existed in medieval Europe

historical novels: stories that are set during historical events

illustrate: provides pictures for a book

library science: the study of libraries

manuscripts: drafts of a story before it is published

media: people who report the news in newspapers, TV, and radio

memoir: a person's written account of his or her own life

pastime: a hobby or entertainment that makes time pass in an enjoyable way

paternal: on the father's side of the family

produced: put on stage

profession: a job

psychiatrist: a doctor who treats disorders of the mind

publishing company: a company that produces books

research: study of a subject to learn facts

Index

Photo Credits

Every reasonable effort has been made to trace ownership and to obtain permission to reprint copyright material. The publishers would be pleased to have any errors or omissions brought to their attention so that they may be corrected in subsequent printings.

Courtesy of Avi: cover, pages 3, 4, 6, 9, 11, 22; **Disney Publishing**: page 21 right; **Courtesy of Christopher Mark Owyoung**: page 10; **Courtesy of Shaun Wolf Wortis**: page 17; **Courtesy of Linda Wright**: pages 1, 16.

$ 26.00

CONNETQUOT PUBLIC LIBRARY
760 Ocean Avenue
Bohemia, NY   11716
631-567-5079

Library Hours:

Monday-Friday	**9:00 - 9:00**
Saturday	**9:00 - 5:00**
Sunday (Oct.-May)	**1:00 - 5:00**

GAYLORD M